WORLD OF ENGINEERING

BUILDING A PLANE

NATALIE HUMPHREY

PowerKiDS press

Published in 2024 by The Rosen Publishing Group, Inc.
2544 Clinton Street, Buffalo, NY 14224

Portions of this work were originally authored by Amy Hayes and published as *How a Plane Is Made.* All new material in this edition was authored by Natalie Humphrey.

Editor: Natalie Humphrey
Designer: Rachel Rising

Photo Credits: Cover, aappp/Shutterstock.com; Cover, pp. 1-24 Alef-Beth/Shutterstock.com; Cover, pp. 1, 3, 22-24 RoseRodionova/Shutterstock.com; Cover, p. 1 Creative Hawk/Shutterstock.com; Cover, pp. 1-24 Artistdesign29/Shutterstock.com; p. 5 dongfang/Shutterstock.com; p. 6 Surasak_Photo/Shutterstock.com; p. 7 Dimitrios Karamitros/Shutterstock.com; p. 9 tratong/Shutterstock.com; p. 11 https://commons.wikimedia.org/wiki/File:MD-11_12ft_Wind_Tunnel_Test.jpg; p. 13 Alhim/Shutterstock.com; p. 14 FrameAngel/Shutterstock.com;p. 15 Nadezda Murmakova/Shutterstock.com; p. 17 frank_peters/Shutterstock.com; p. 18 Kitthanes/Shutterstock.com; p. 19 Skycolors/Shutterstock.com; pp. 20, 21 Intellson/Shutterstock.com; p. 20 noir_illustration/Shutterstock.com; p. 21 Foreverbung/Shutterstock.com.

Library of Congress Cataloging-in-Publication Data

Names: Humphrey, Natalie, author.
Title: Building a plane / Natalie Humphrey.
Description: Buffalo, New York : PowerKids Press, [2024] | Series: World of engineering | Includes index.
Identifiers: LCCN 2023015779 (print) | LCCN 2023015780 (ebook) | ISBN 9781642826470 (library binding) | ISBN 9781642826463 (paperback) | ISBN 9781642826487 (ebook)
Subjects: LCSH: Airplanes--Design and construction--Juvenile literature. | Aeronautics--Juvenile literature. | CYAC: Airplanes. | Aeronautics.
Classification: LCC TL547 .H7949 2024 (print) | LCC TL547 (ebook) | DDC 629.133/34--dc23/eng/20230419
LC record available at https://lccn.loc.gov/2023015779
LC ebook record available at https://lccn.loc.gov/2023015780

Manufactured in the United States of America

CPSIA Compliance Information: Batch #CSPK24. For Further Information contact Rosen Publishing at 1-800-237-9932.

CONTENTS

FLYING THROUGH THE AIR

One of the safest and fastest ways to get from place to place is with an airplane! People use airplanes every day to get where they need to go all around the world. Some airplanes are big enough for only one or two people. The largest planes, called jumbo jets, are big enough to carry hundreds of people.

But how do airplanes get into the air? What does it take to build an airplane? Science and **engineering**!

ENGINEERING WONDERS

In 1903, the Wright brothers flew the first powered airplane. Our planes today might look very different from theirs, but they used the same science to fly!

IN 2022, THERE WERE OVER 200,000 AIRPLANES IN THE UNITED STATES ALONE.

To get and stay in the air, airplanes use different forces. The first force is called thrust. Thrust is the force that moves the plane forward. The plane needs to be moving very quickly to get into the air.

Wind moving on top of the wing moves faster than the wind moving under the wing. The pressure, or force that pushes on something else, from the air creates a force called lift. Lift is the force that pushes the plane into the air!

ENGINEERING WONDERS

Airplane engineers study physics to create airplanes. Physics teaches us how forces such as lift and thrust make objects move.

WHEN A PLANE IS FLYING, A FORCE CALLED **DRAG** PULLS IT BACK.

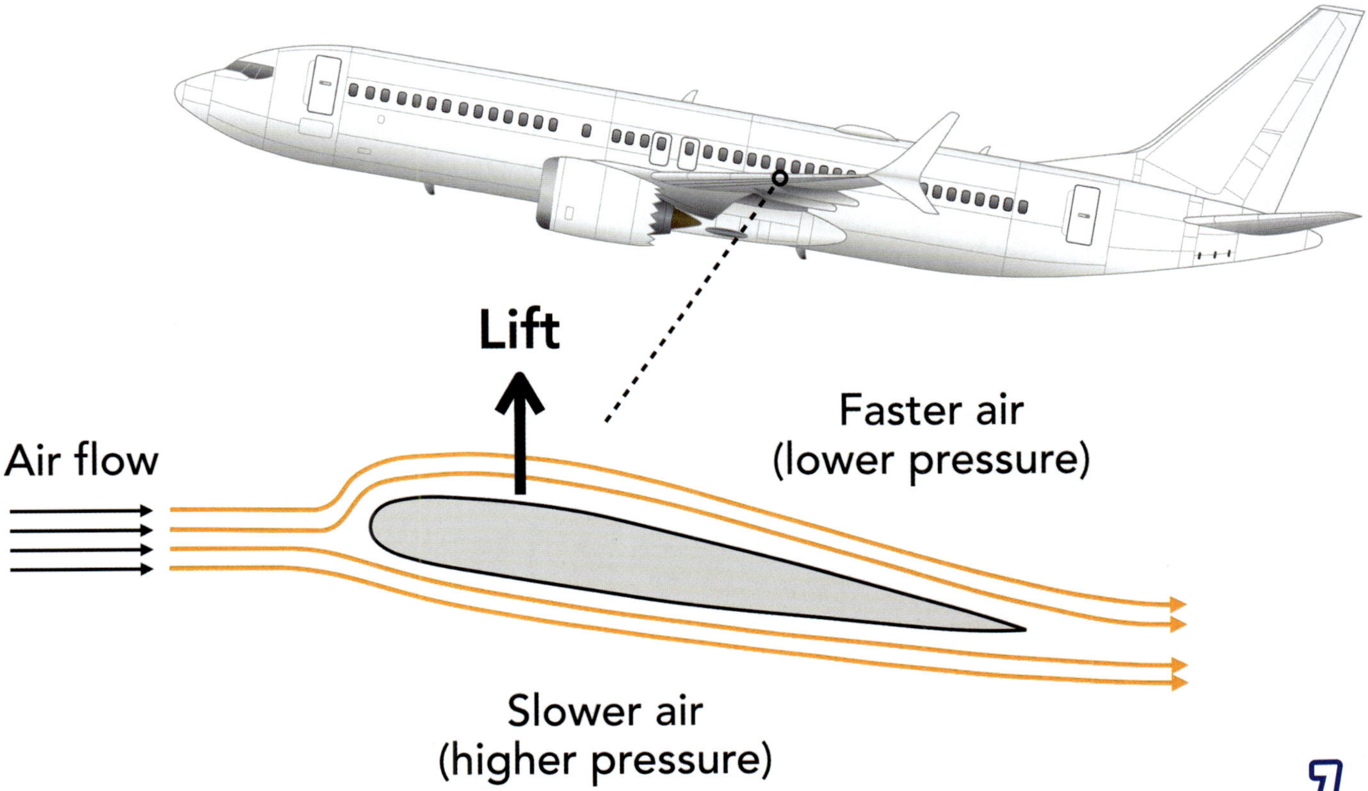

DESIGNING AN AIRPLANE

It takes many people to make an airplane. Engineers work together to come up with the best ideas to make planes fly. A large plane can have hundreds of engineers working to **design** it!

Experts design every single part of a plane. There are chair experts, wing experts, and engine experts. Before building a new plane, the experts work together for years. This is to make sure that the new plane is as safe as it can be.

ENGINEERING WONDERS

When engineers design a plane, they also think about the airports the plane will land in. This is to make sure a plane is the right shape and size for the airport!

LARGE PLANES SUCH AS JUMBO JETS CAN LAND ONLY IN SPECIAL AIRPORTS.

Once part of an airplane is designed, it's time to test it. Each part of a plane must be tested by itself before it can be put together with the other pieces. This is to make sure each part can handle all sorts of **situations**.

To test the parts, engineers use computer **simulations** and wind-tunnel models. Sometimes, engineers will even make a small model of the new plane to test it! If a part fails one of its tests, engineers change the part's design and test it again.

ENGINEERING WONDERS

What is a wind tunnel? Wind tunnels are usually long tubes with a powerful fan on one side. The fan blows air at high speeds over whatever the engineers need to test.

WIND TUNNELS AREN'T JUST USED BY AIRPLANE ENGINEERS. CAR MAKERS AND NASA ALSO USE THEM!

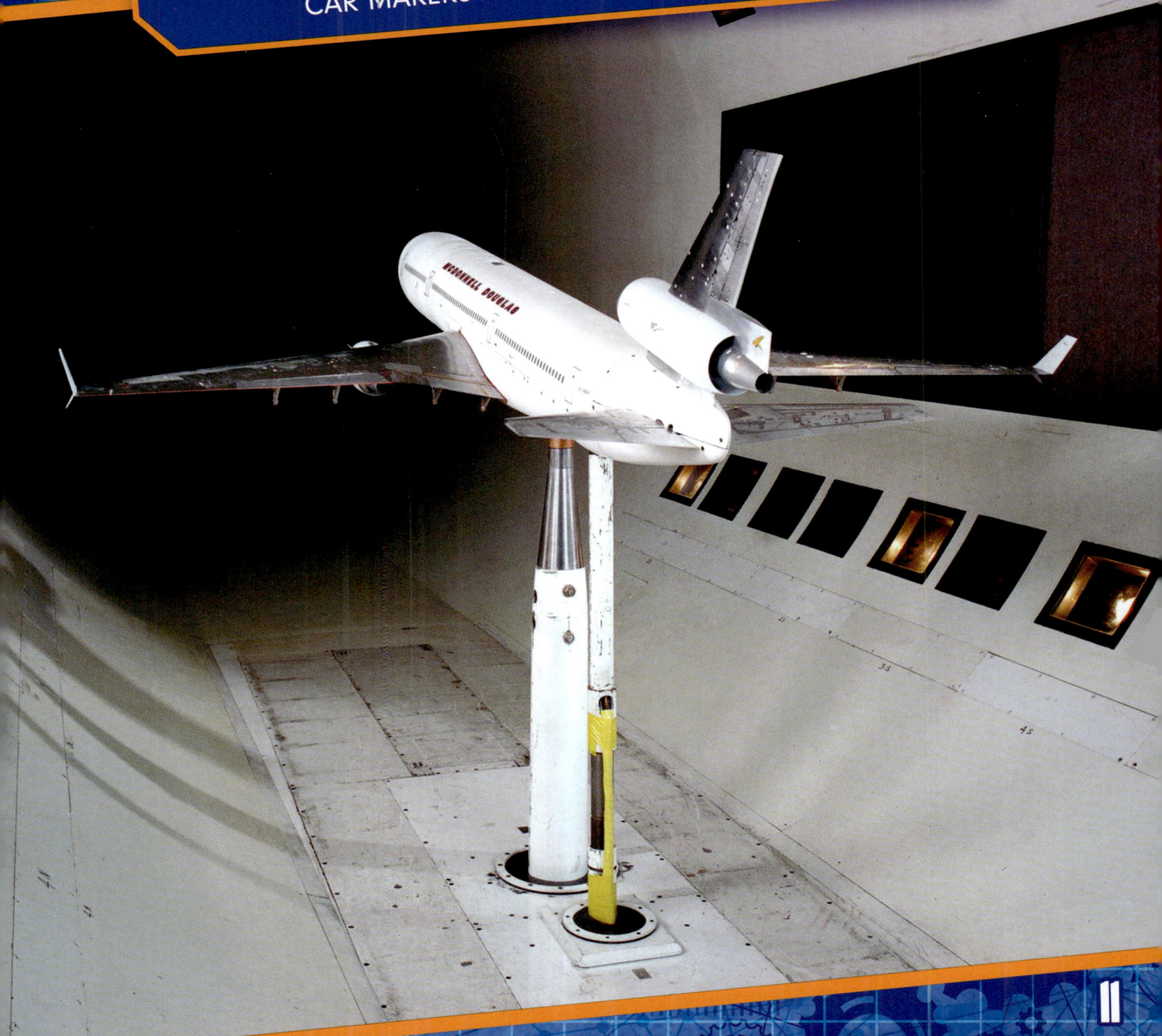

CREATING THE AIRPLANE

It takes a lot of work to make a plane. Smaller airplanes can be **manufactured** in one place. These smaller airplanes can hold only one or two people. Bigger airplanes have a lot of parts! Some of the parts are made at different places and shipped to where the plane is being built.

Once all the parts from other places are brought in, it's time to bring them to the hangar. The hangar is a big building where planes are put together and stored.

ENGINEERING WONDERS

The hangars used for bigger airplanes can be huge. The hangar where Boeing's 747 plane is manufactured is so tall sometimes clouds form inside!

THE BOEING 747 HAS OVER 6 MILLION PARTS.

One of the most important parts of an airplane are the wings! A wing's frame is made of many parts that need to be as strong and light as possible. The frame consists of a rear spar, main spar, and the ribs.

Workers use a special kind of tape to cover the tops and bottoms of the wings. But before the tape can be put on the wings, they need to be baked!

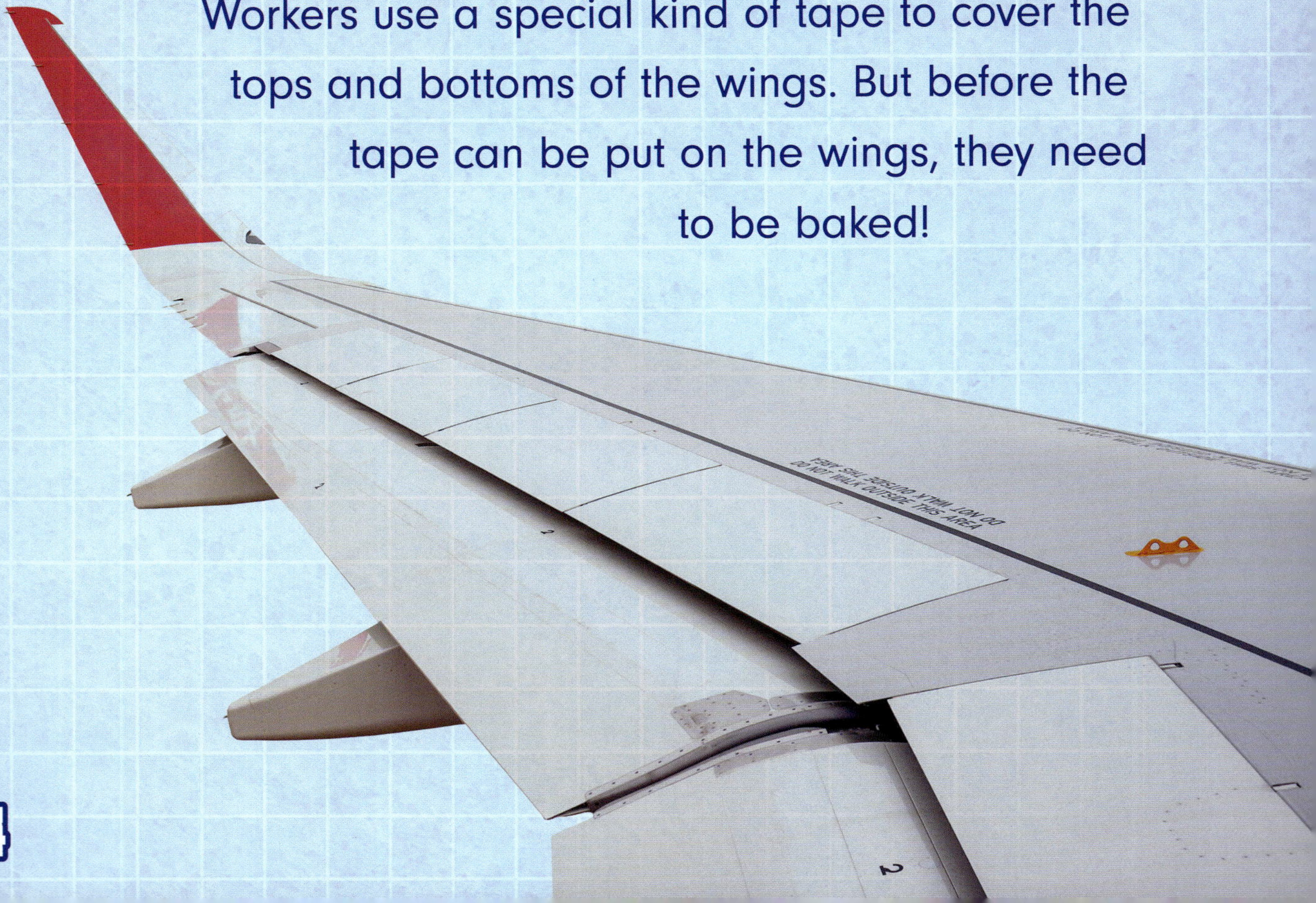

ENGINEERING WONDERS

The spars are like the skeleton of the plane's wings. Most planes have at least two spars that are made from metals such as **aluminum**.

THE FUSELAGE

The fuselage (FYOO-suh-lazh) is where people sit in an airplane. The fuselage is the shape of a long tube. The pilots sit in the front of the fuselage in a closed space called the cockpit. This is where pilots control the plane.

In the newest planes, the fuselage is made of composite **materials**. These are materials made of many different things. One example is carbon fiber. Carbon fiber is made of many threads of different materials **woven** together. It's very light and strong.

ENGINEERING WONDERS

To keep a plane from falling over when it's on the ground, workers need to make sure it's balanced. Wheels, which help a plane land and take off, are put under the fuselage so the plane doesn't tip over.

THE WHEELS ARE JOINED TO A PART CALLED THE LANDING GEAR.

PUTTING THE PLANE TOGETHER

After workers make all the parts, they're ready to put the plane together. Since planes are heavy and can be big, workers need to use cranes to put the pieces in place. Builders join the front and back—called the nose and tail—to the fuselage.

They add the wings and then the landing gear next. When everything else is on, workers finally add the engines. After the engines are on, it's time to test the airplane!

ENGINEERING WONDERS

When new planes are designed, engineers test them out in every flight condition. This is to make sure they are safe before more are made.

BUILDERS **WELD** OR **RIVET** MANY AIRPLANE PIECES TOGETHER.

MAKE YOUR OWN PAPER AIRPLANE

Now that we know how airplanes work, it's time to make our own paper airplane!

WHAT YOU NEED

▸ paper ◂

HOW TO

1. Fold a piece of paper in half **vertically**. Then unfold the paper with the fold facing down.

2. Fold two opposite corners to the middle fold of the paper.

3. Flip the paper over. Fold the top two corners towards the center fold again. This should make sharper point.

4. Fold the paper in half against the vertical fold.

5. Fold the corners down to make your plane's wings.

6. Make sure your folds are even.

7. Throw your paper airplane and see if it flies!

GLOSSARY

aluminum: A type of lightweight but strong metal.

design: To create the plan for something.

drag: A force generated by the movement of a solid object through a fluid or gas that works to slow the forward motion of the solid object.

engineering: The study and practice of using math and science to do useful things, such as building machines.

expert: Someone with special skills or knowledge gained from training.

manufacture: To create products in a factory, usually with machines.

material: Something from which something else can be made.

simulation: The representation of the functioning of one system or process by means of another system.

situations: All the facts, conditions, and events that affect someone or something in a certain time and place.

rivet: To connect two pieces of metal together using a metal bolt with a head at one end and a piece that is flattened into a head on the other end.

weld: To join two pieces of metal together by melting them.

woven: Having to do with a kind of material made by weaving, or the way of making something by overlapping thread, cloth, or other matter.

vertical: Going straight up or down.

FOR MORE INFORMATION

BOOKS

Amoroso, Cynthia. *Airplanes*. Parker, CO: The Child's World, 2023.

Rogers, Marie. *Giant Jumbo Jets*. Buffalo, NY: PowerKids Press, 2022.

Schuh, Mari C. *Airplanes*. Minnetonka, MN: Kaleidoscope Publishing, 2023.

WEBSITES

How Things Fly
www.howthingsfly.si.edu/
Check out interesting videos and fun activities, and learn more about how airplanes work.

National Geographic Kids
www.natgeokids.com/uk/discover/science/general-science/science-dr-karl-planes-fly/
Learn more about how planes work.

Publisher's note to educators and parents: Our editors have carefully reviewed these websites to ensure that they are suitable for students. Many websites change frequently, however, and we cannot guarantee that a site's future contents will continue to meet our high standards of quality and educational value. Be advised that students should be closely supervised whenever they access the internet.

INDEX